TALES · FROM SHAKESPEARE

ILLUSTRATED · BY · ARTHUR · RACKHAM

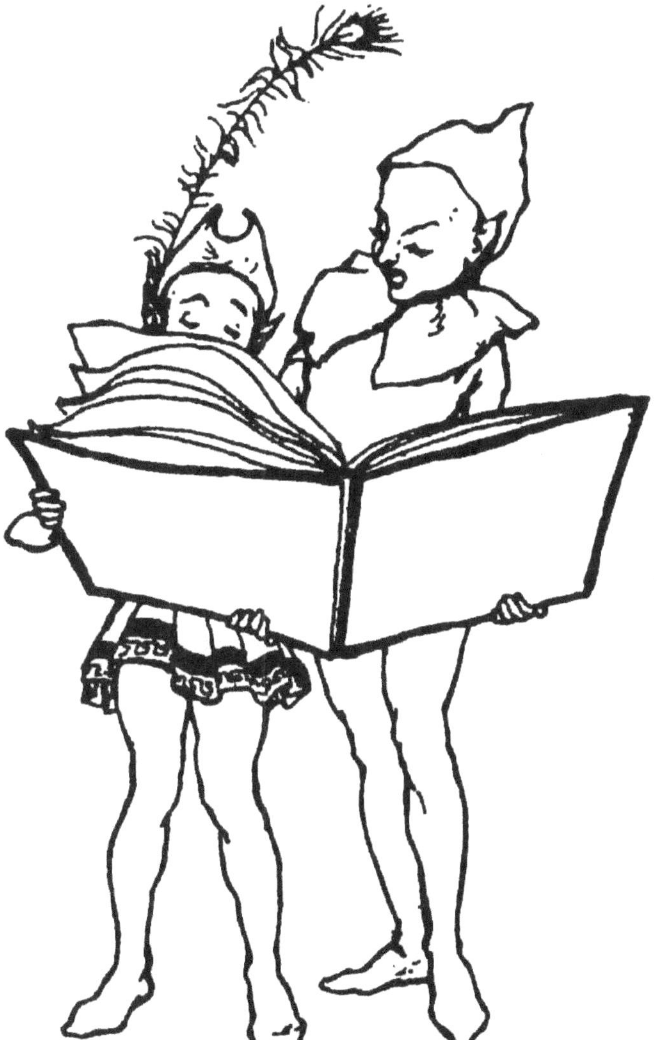

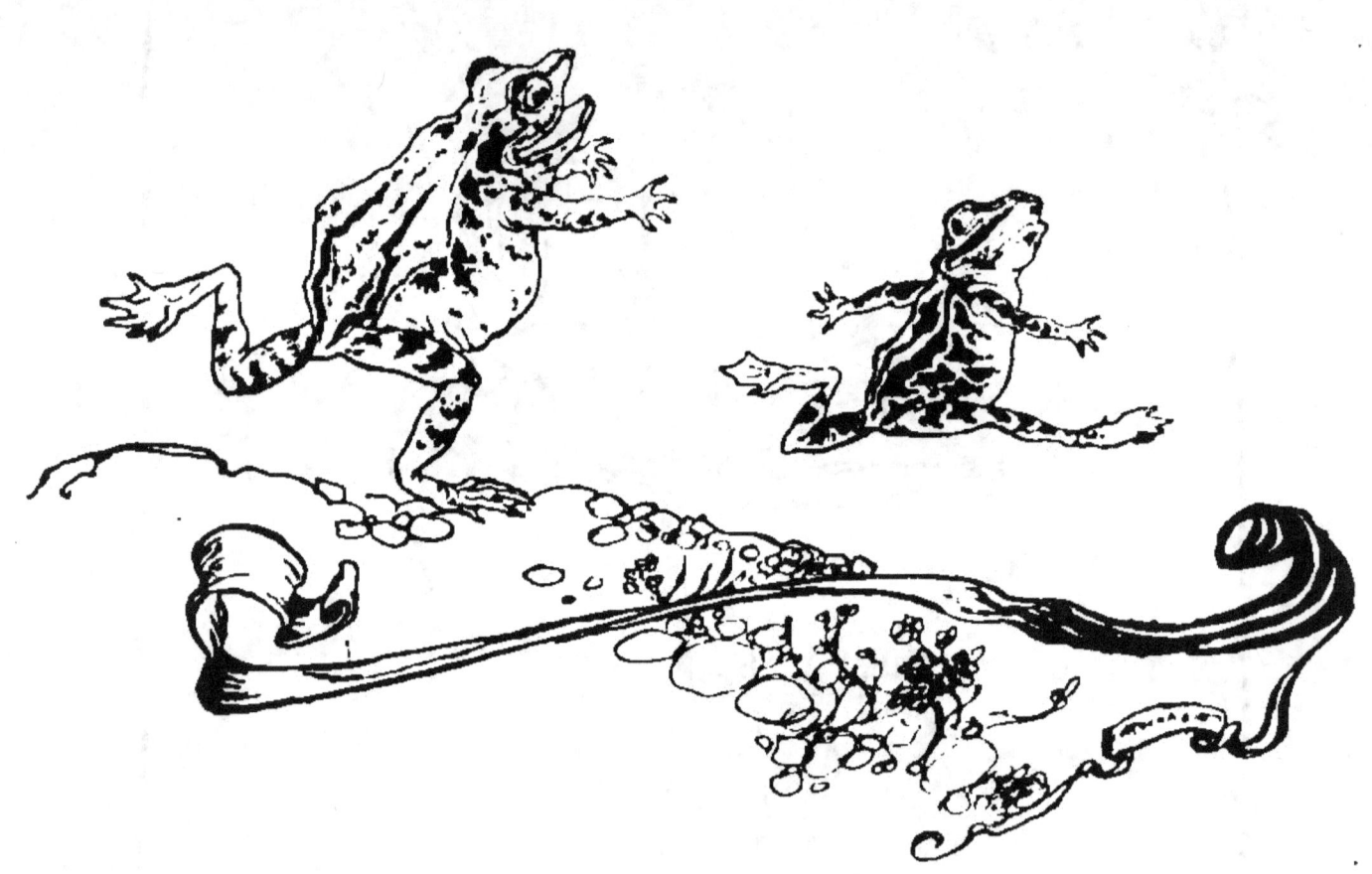

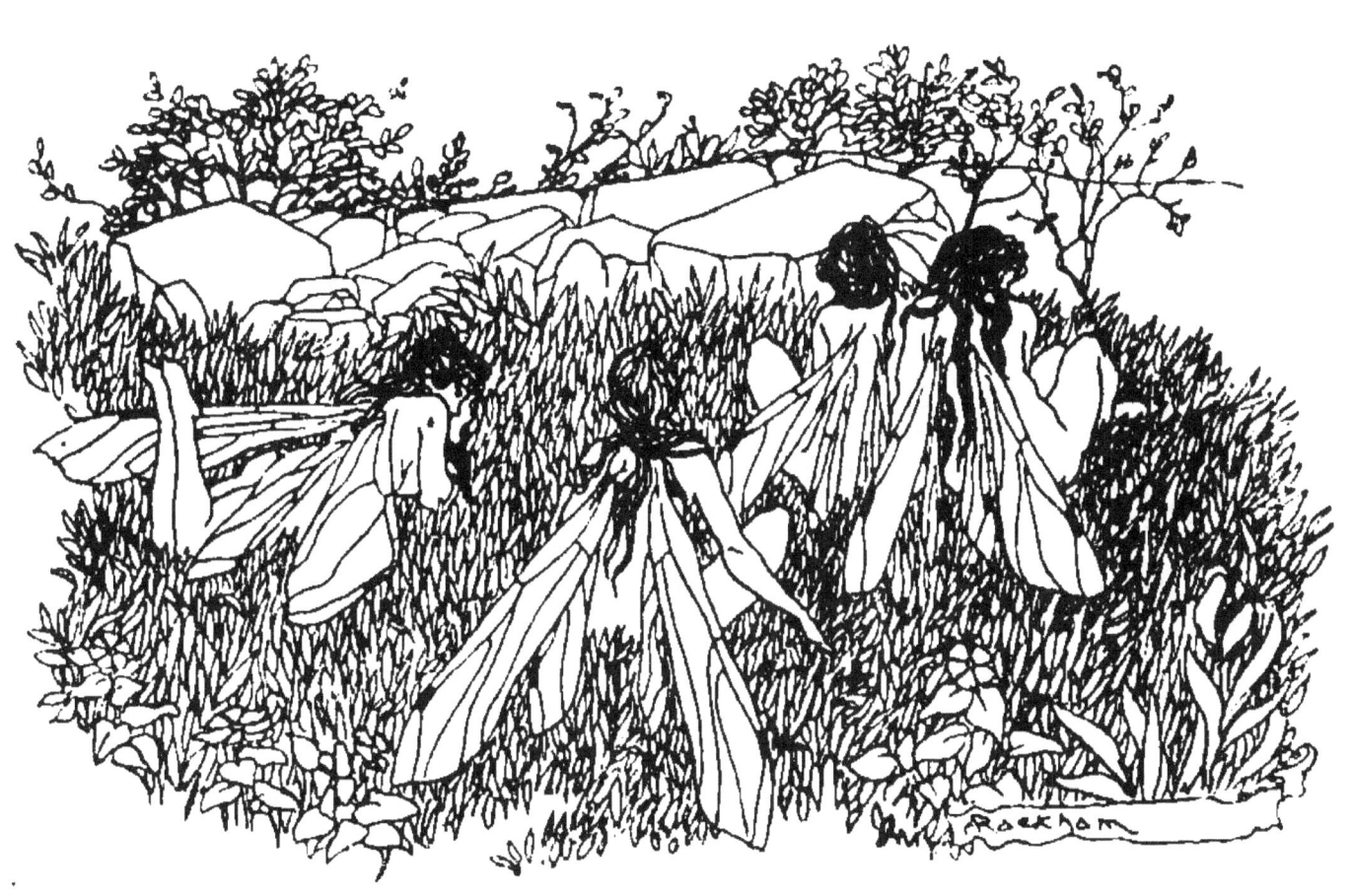

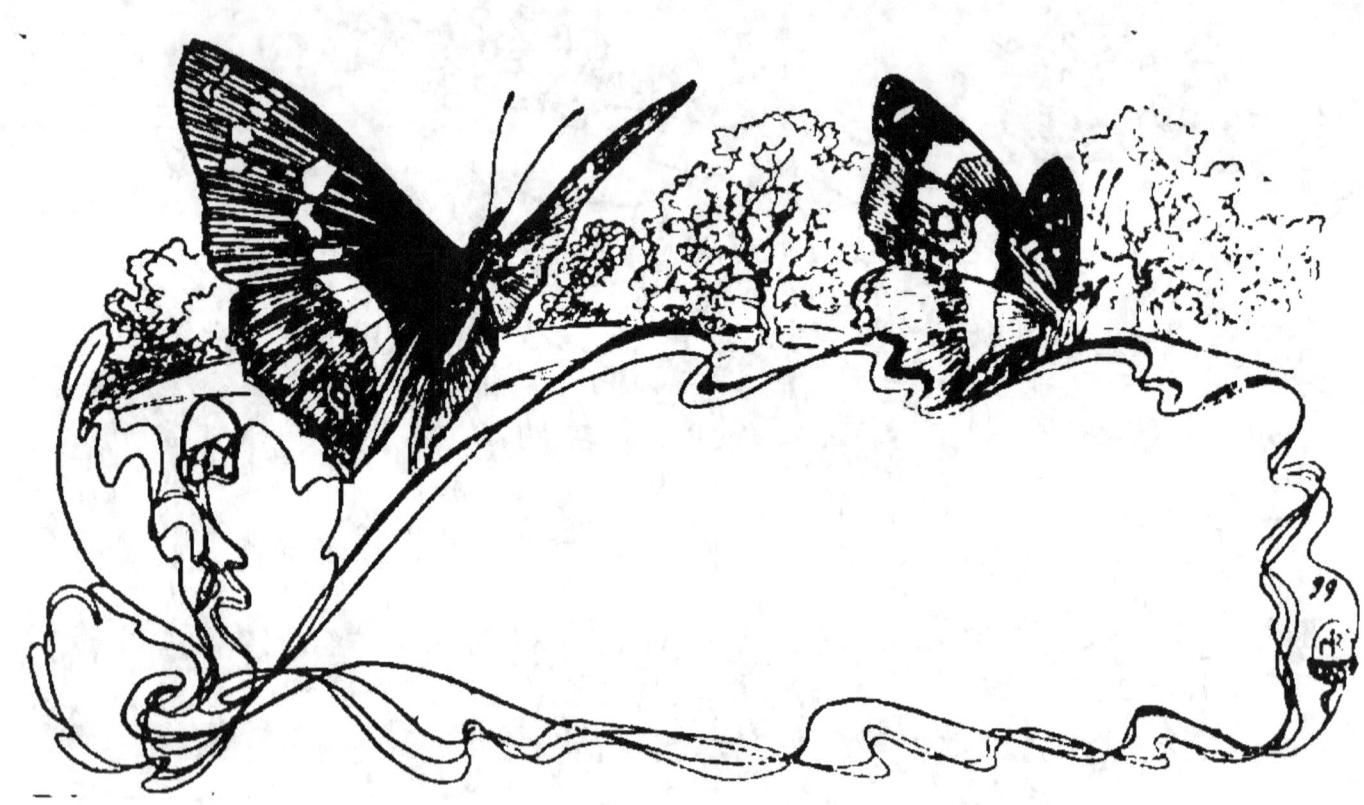

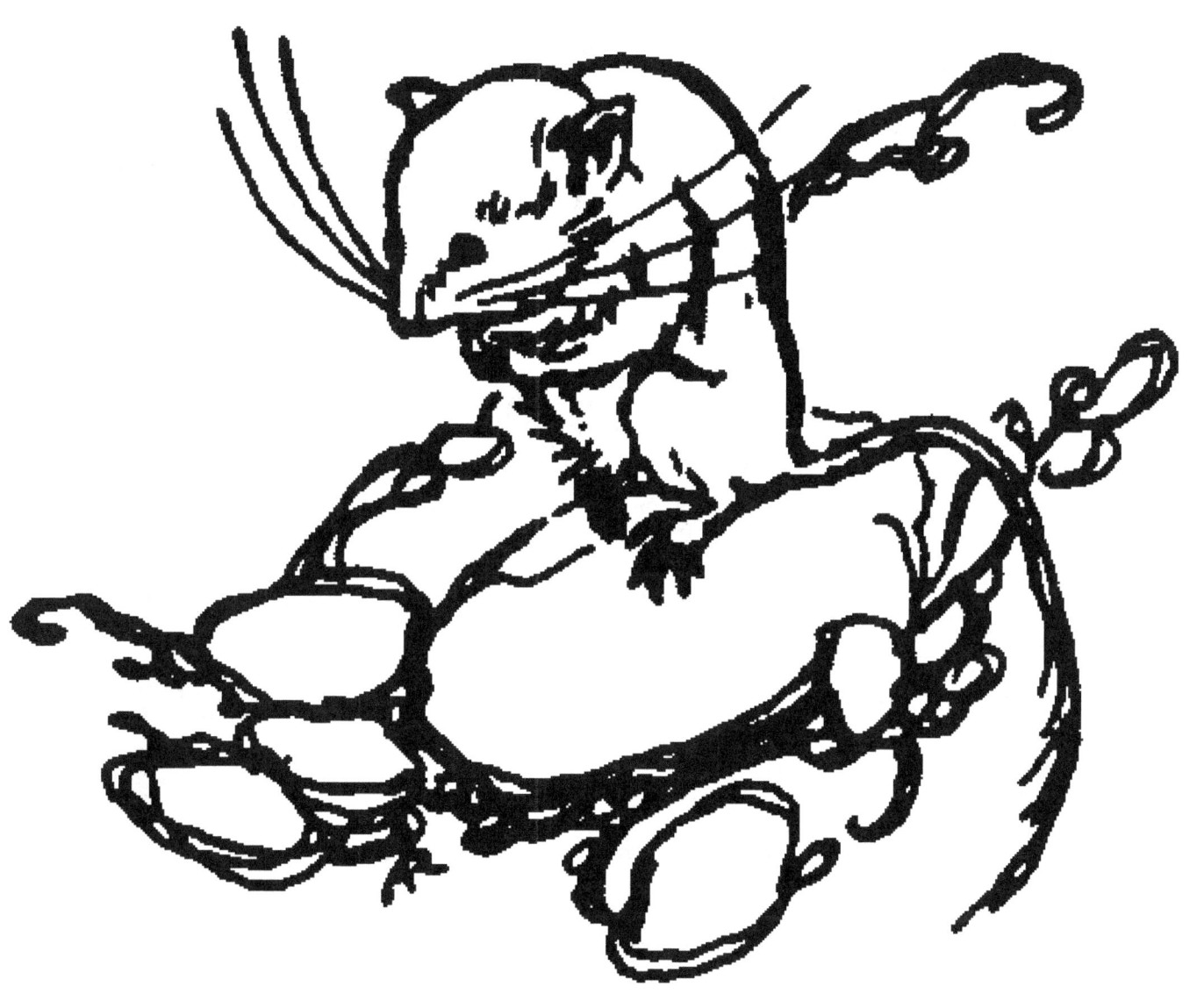

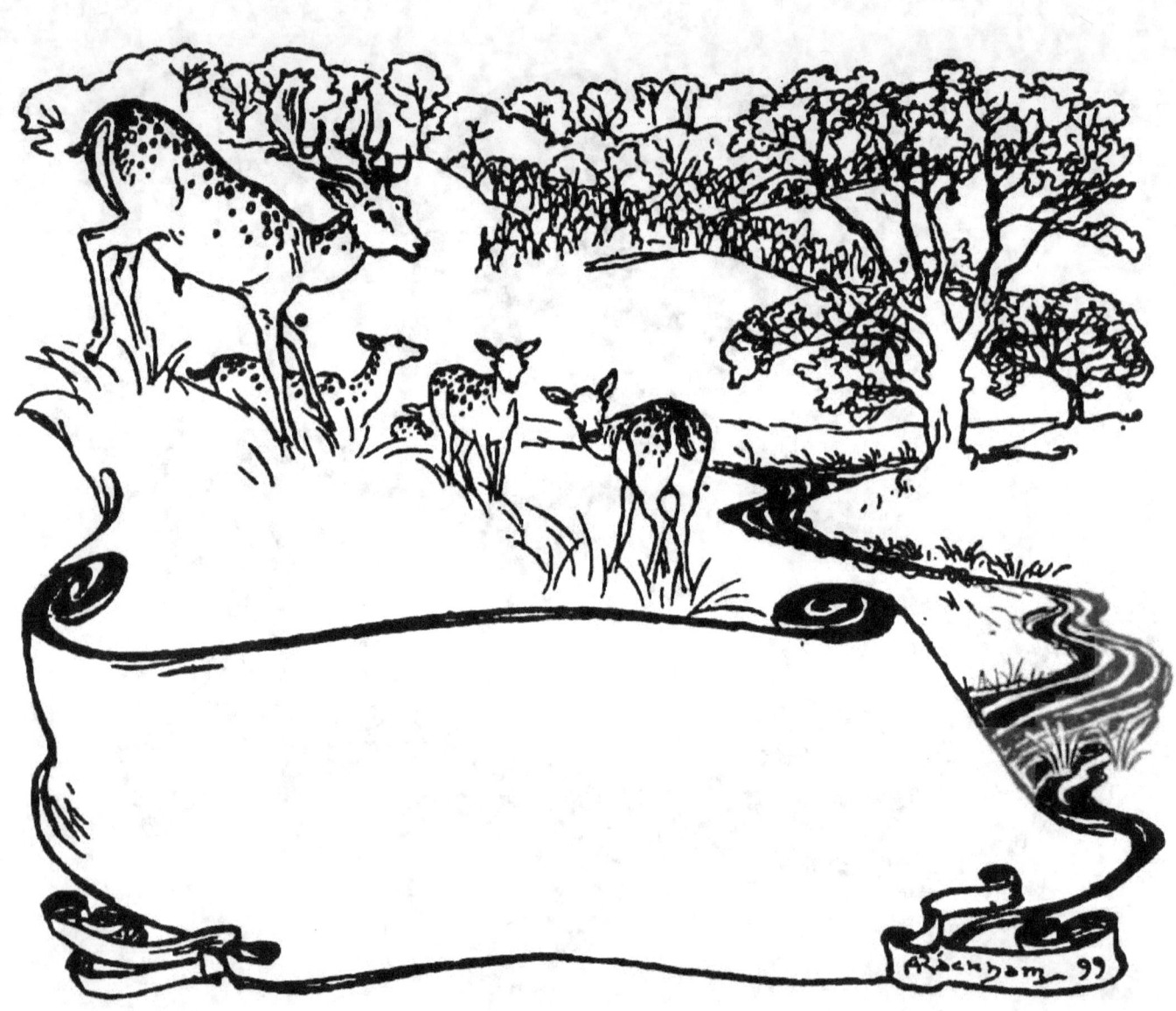

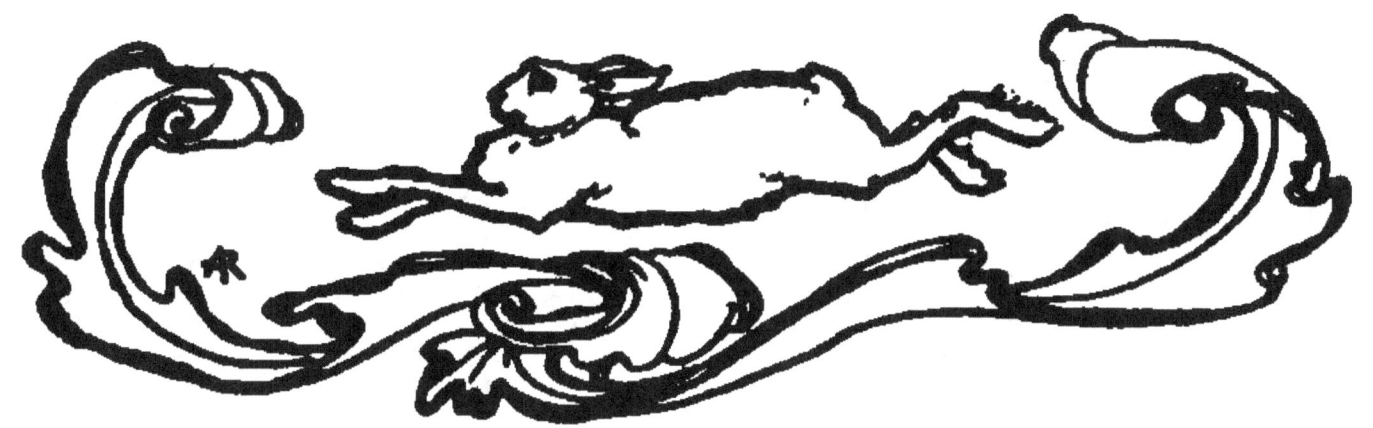

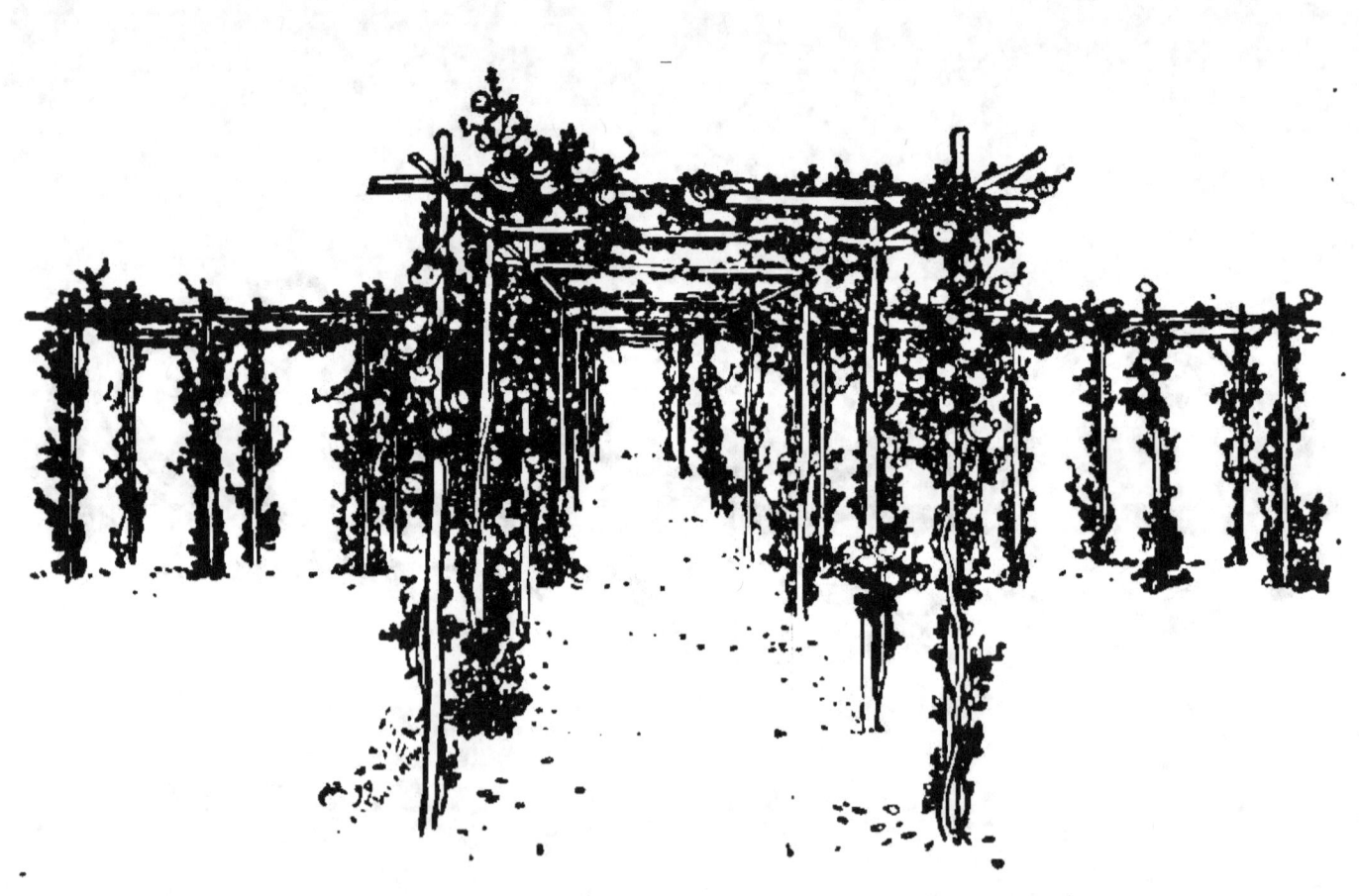

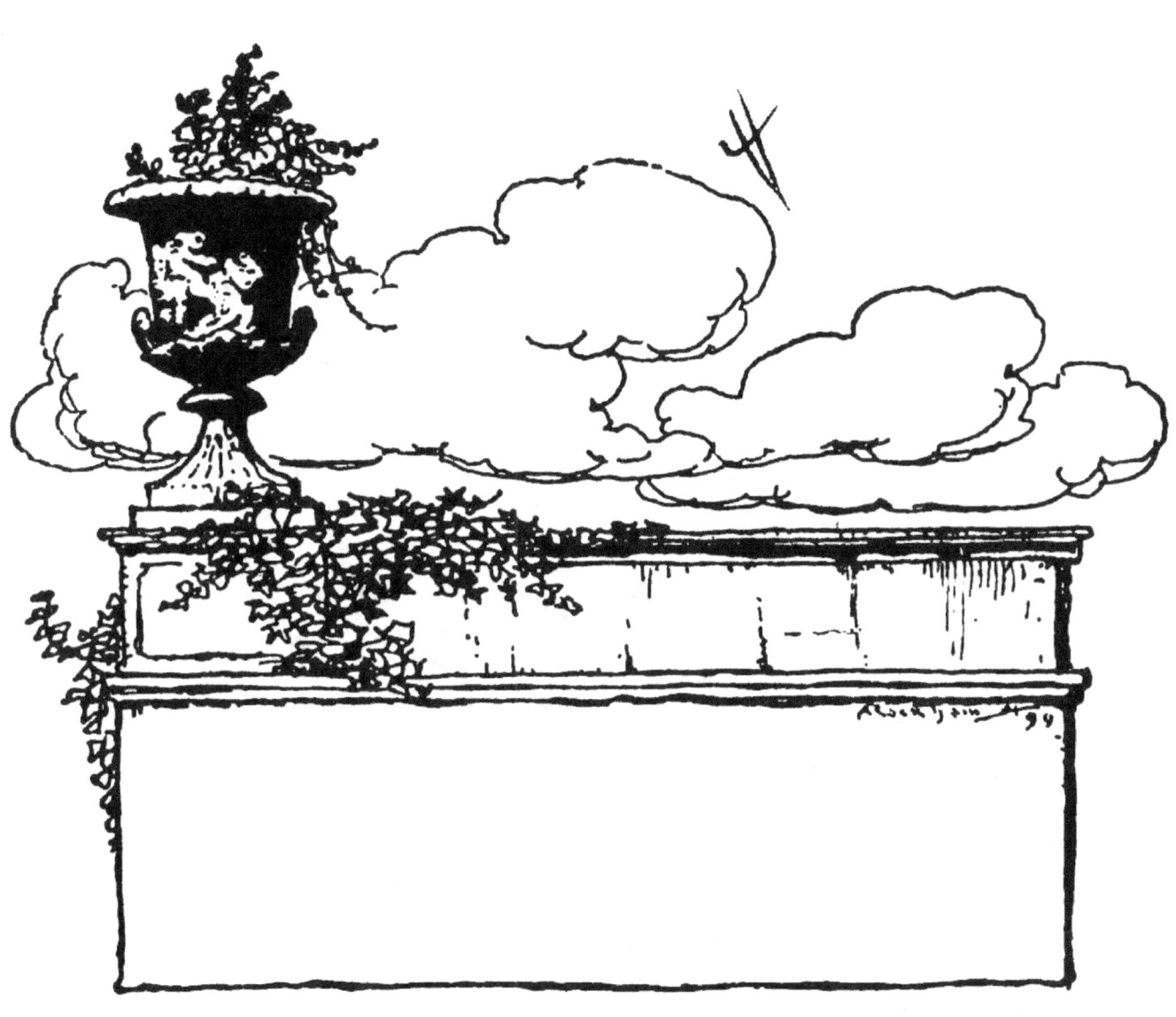

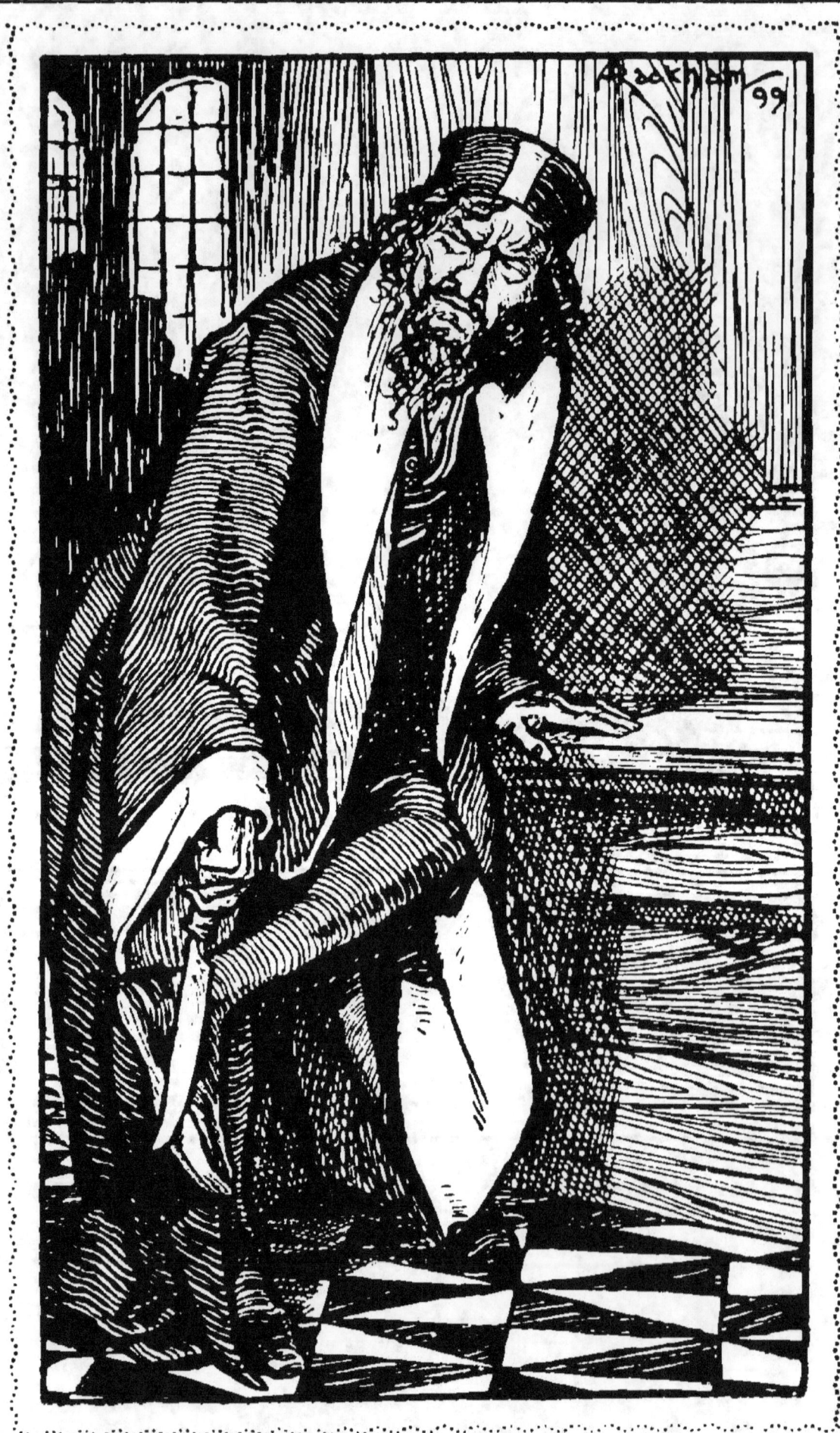

SHYLOCK WAS SHARPENING A LONG KNIFE

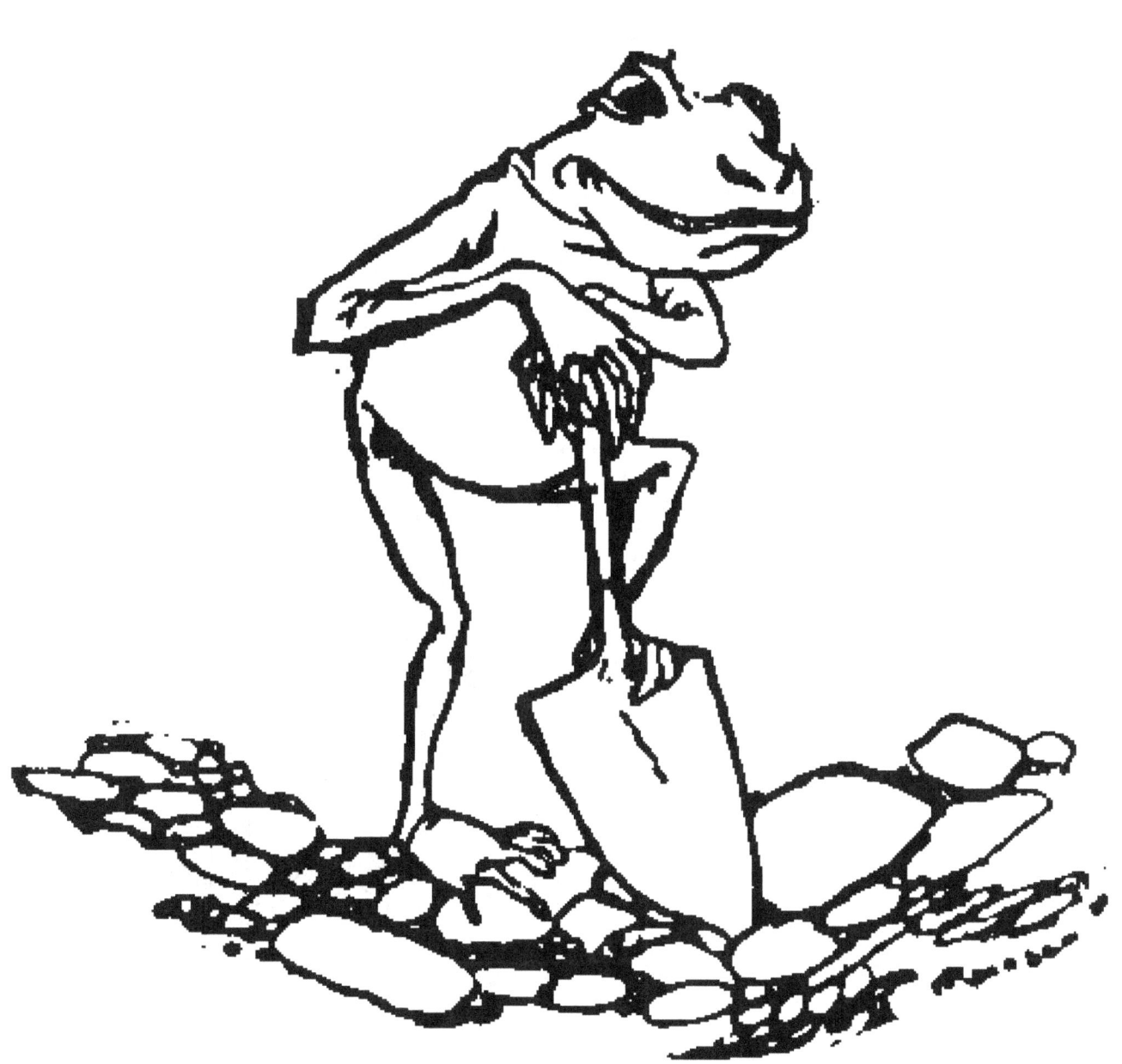

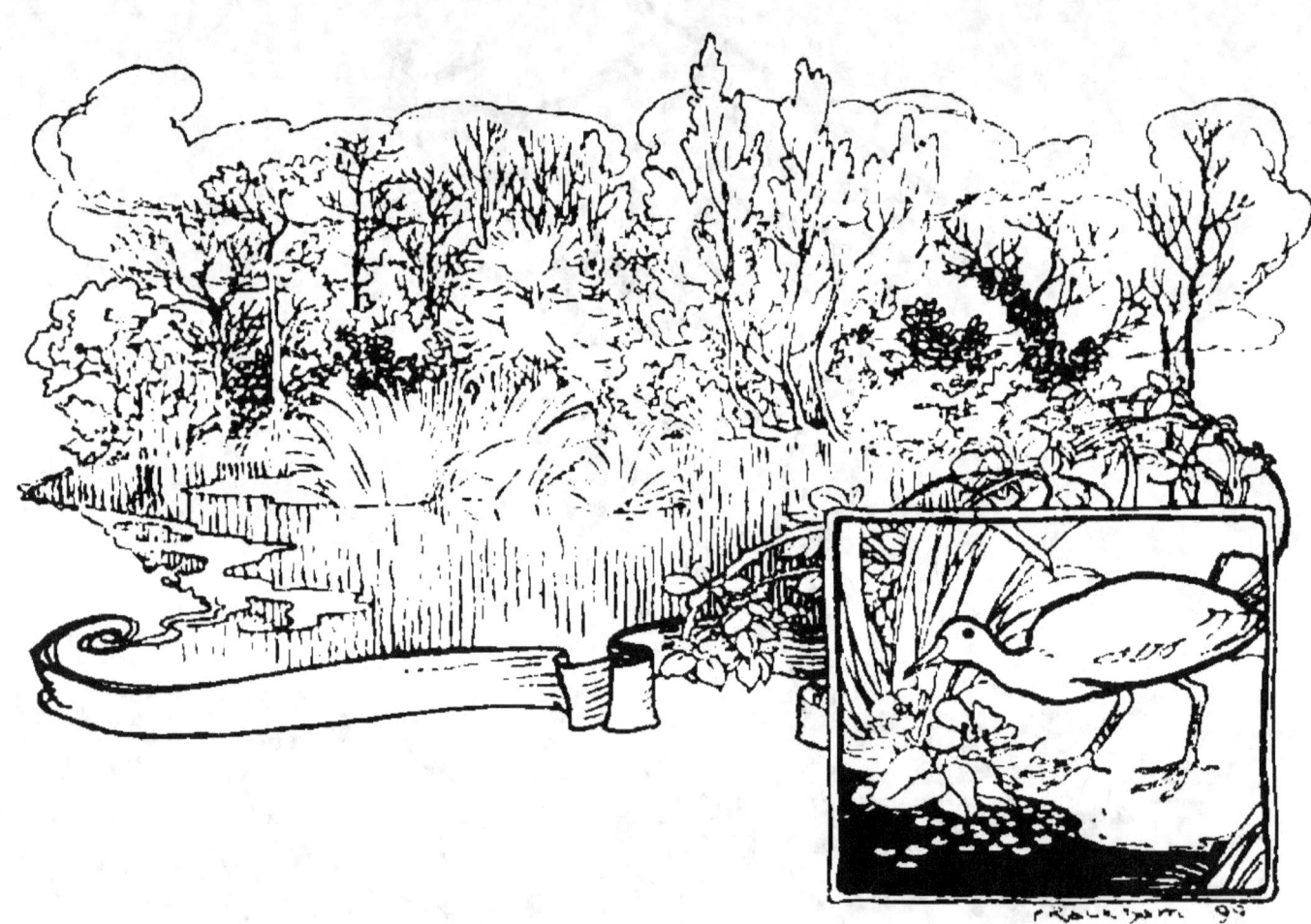

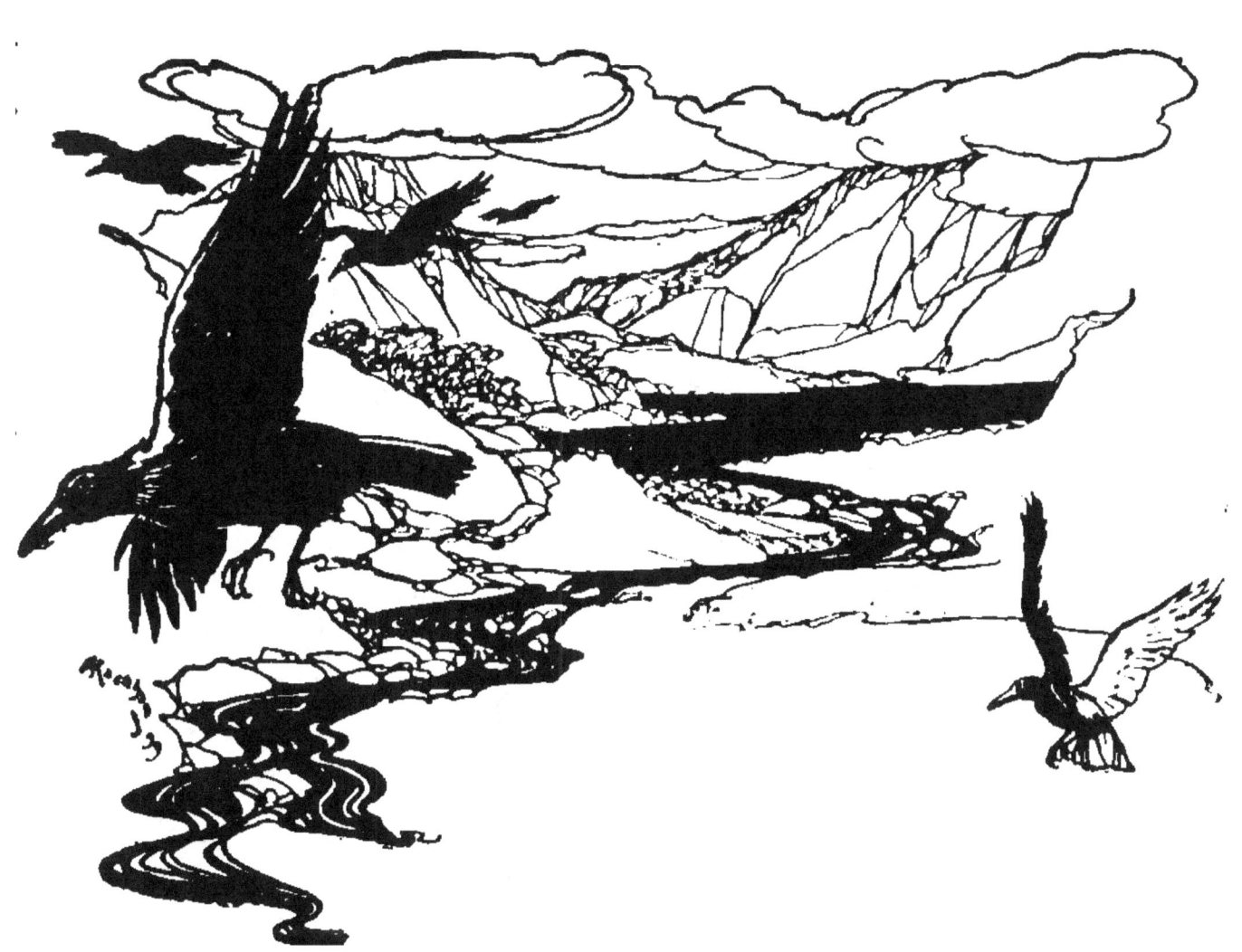

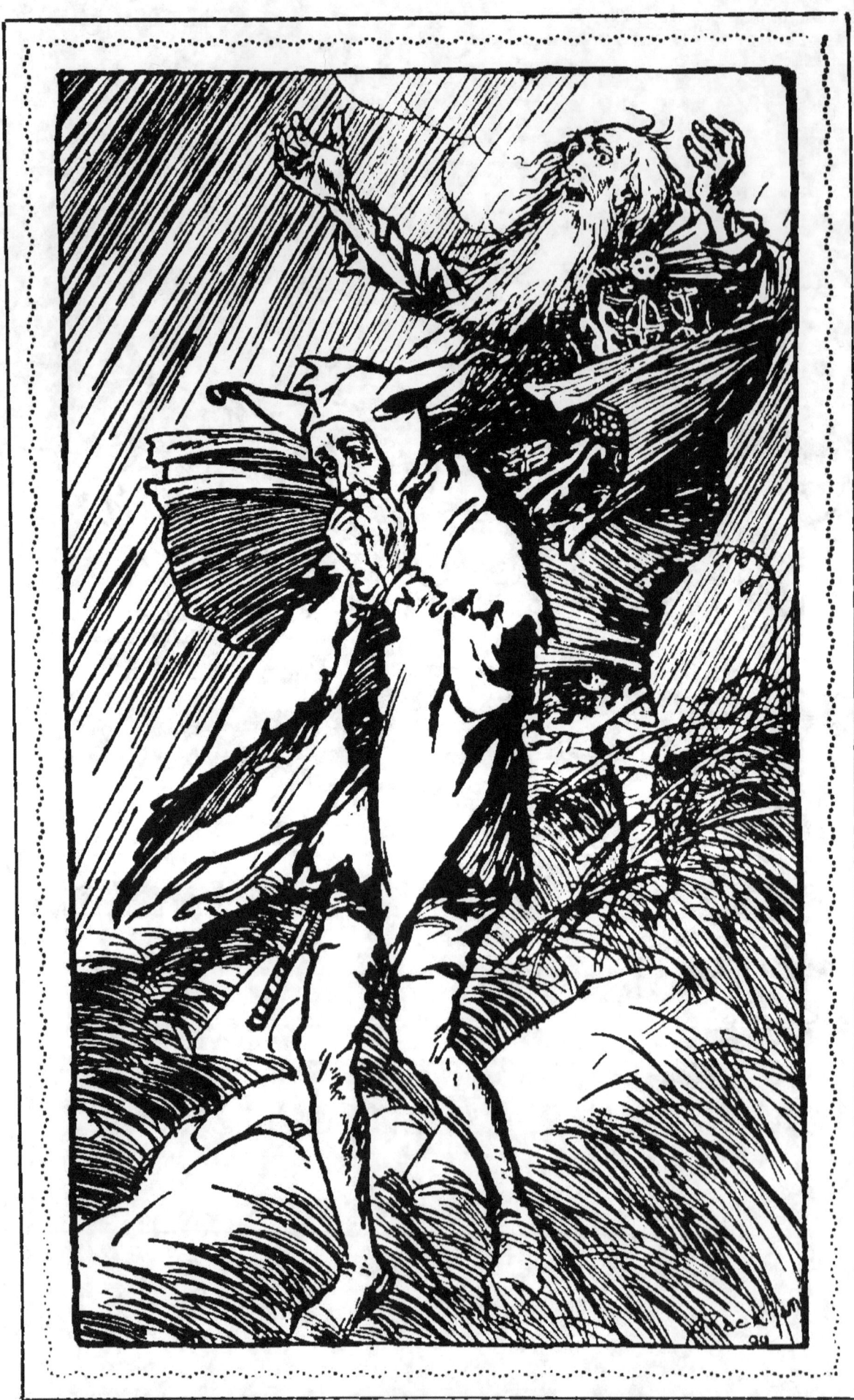

THERE UPON A HEATH, EXPOSED TO THE FURY OF THE STORM ON A DARK NIGHT, DID KING LEAR WANDER OUT

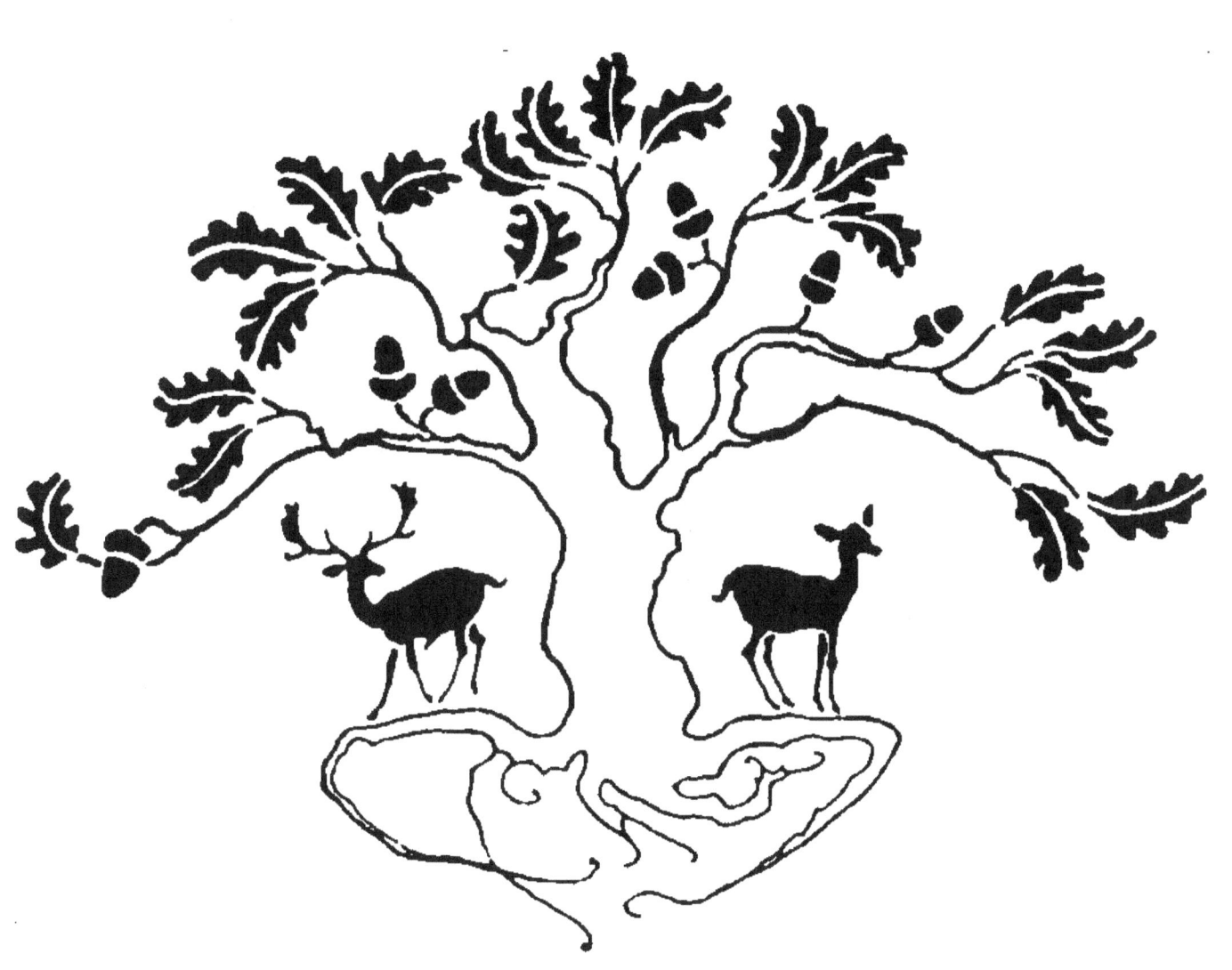

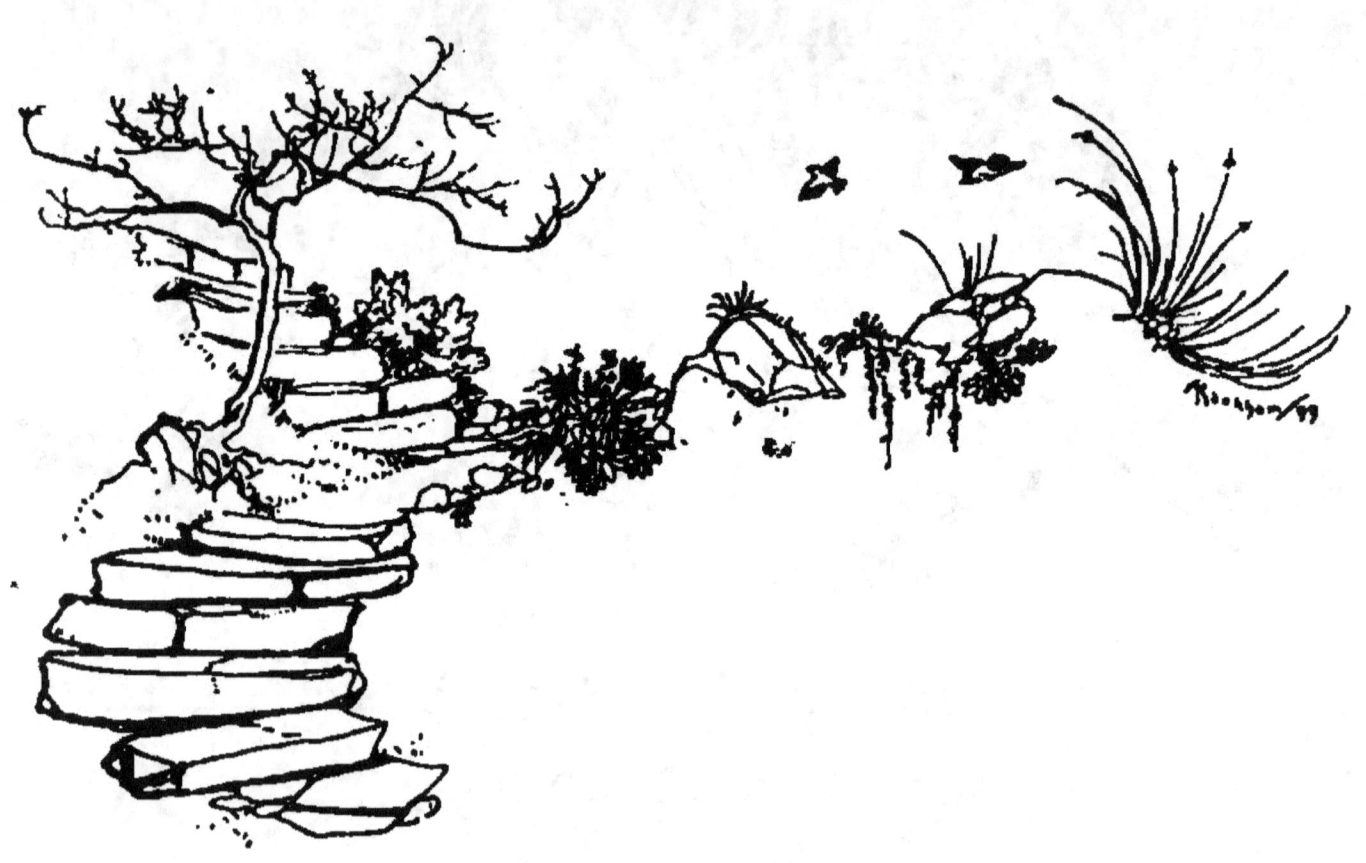

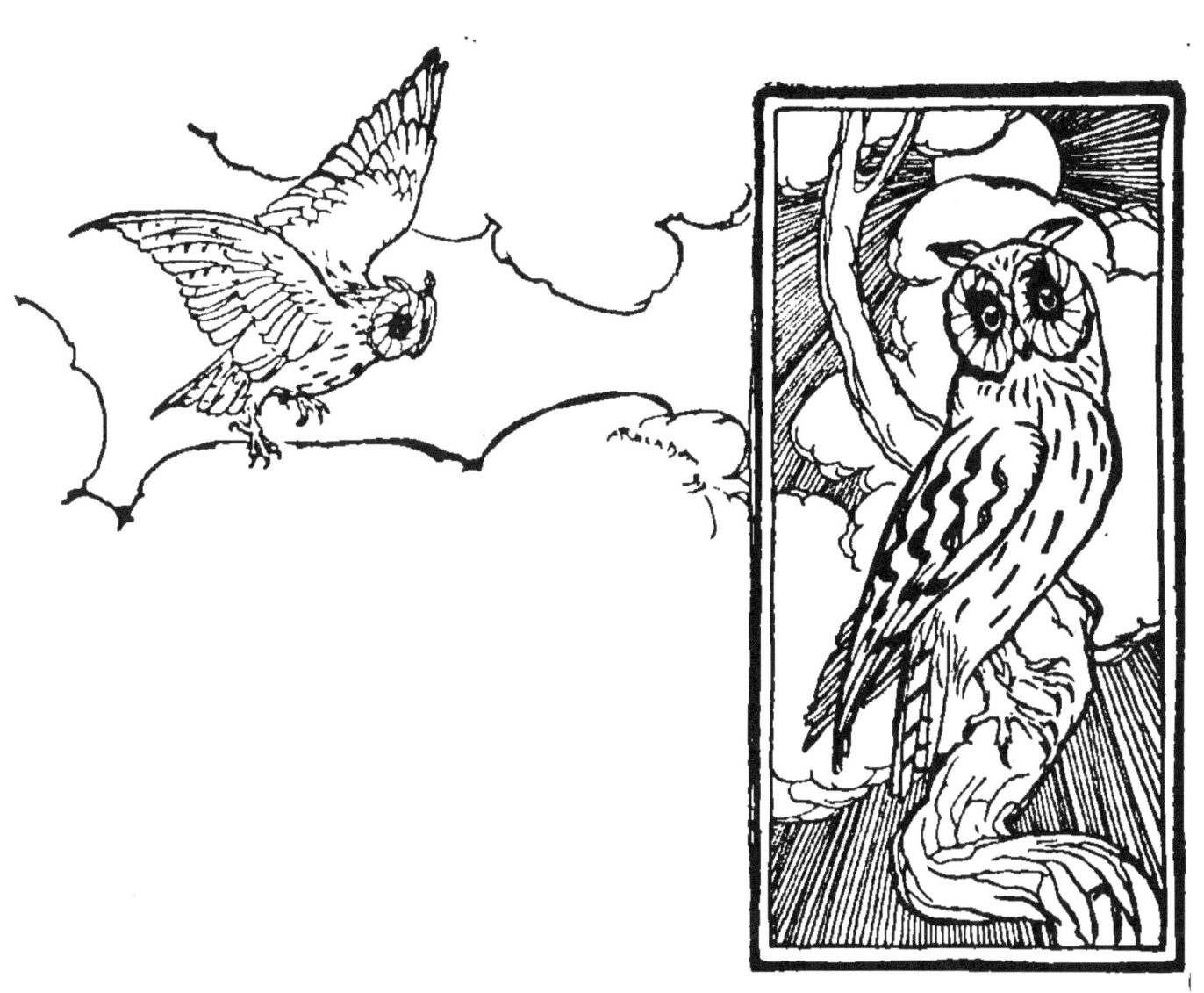

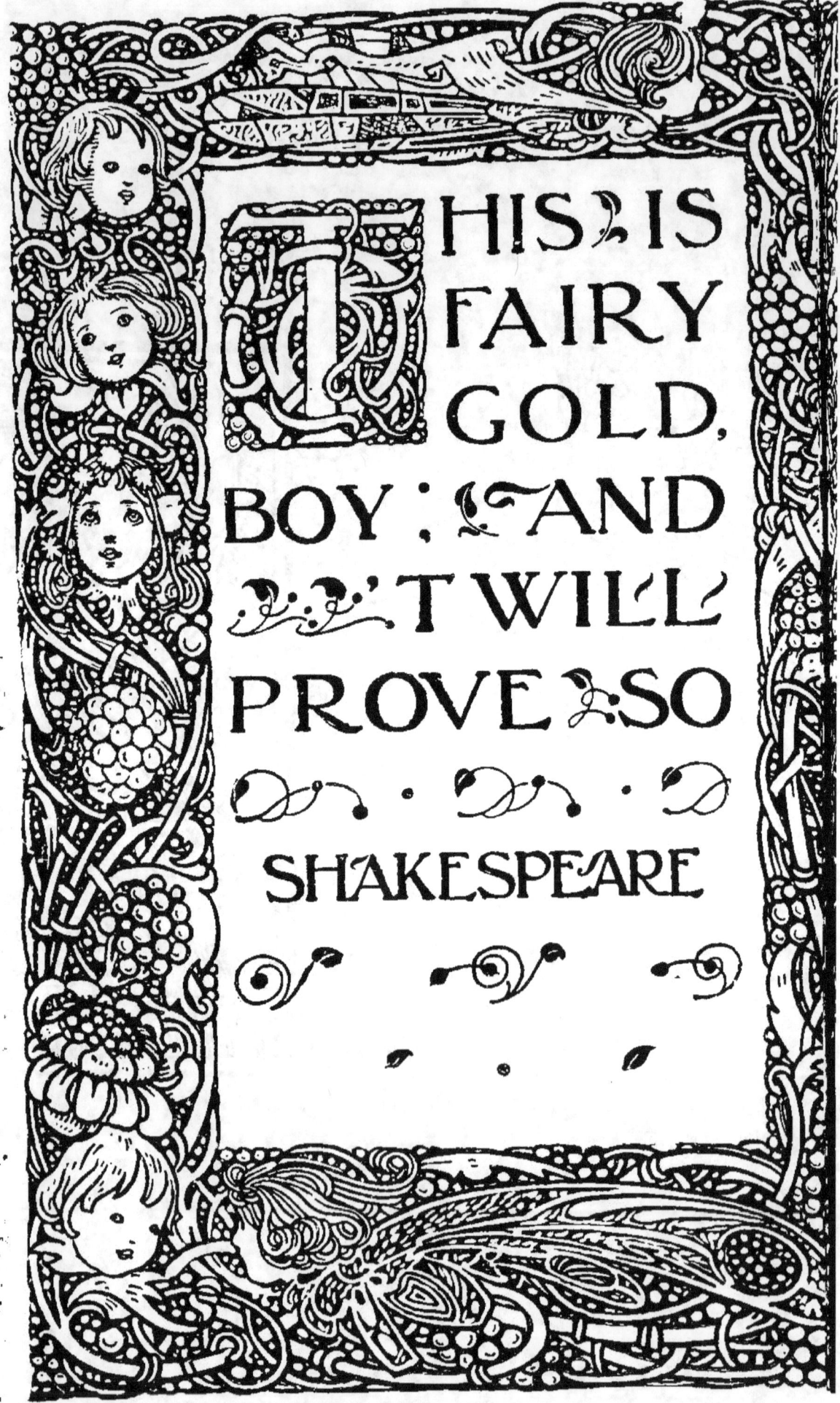

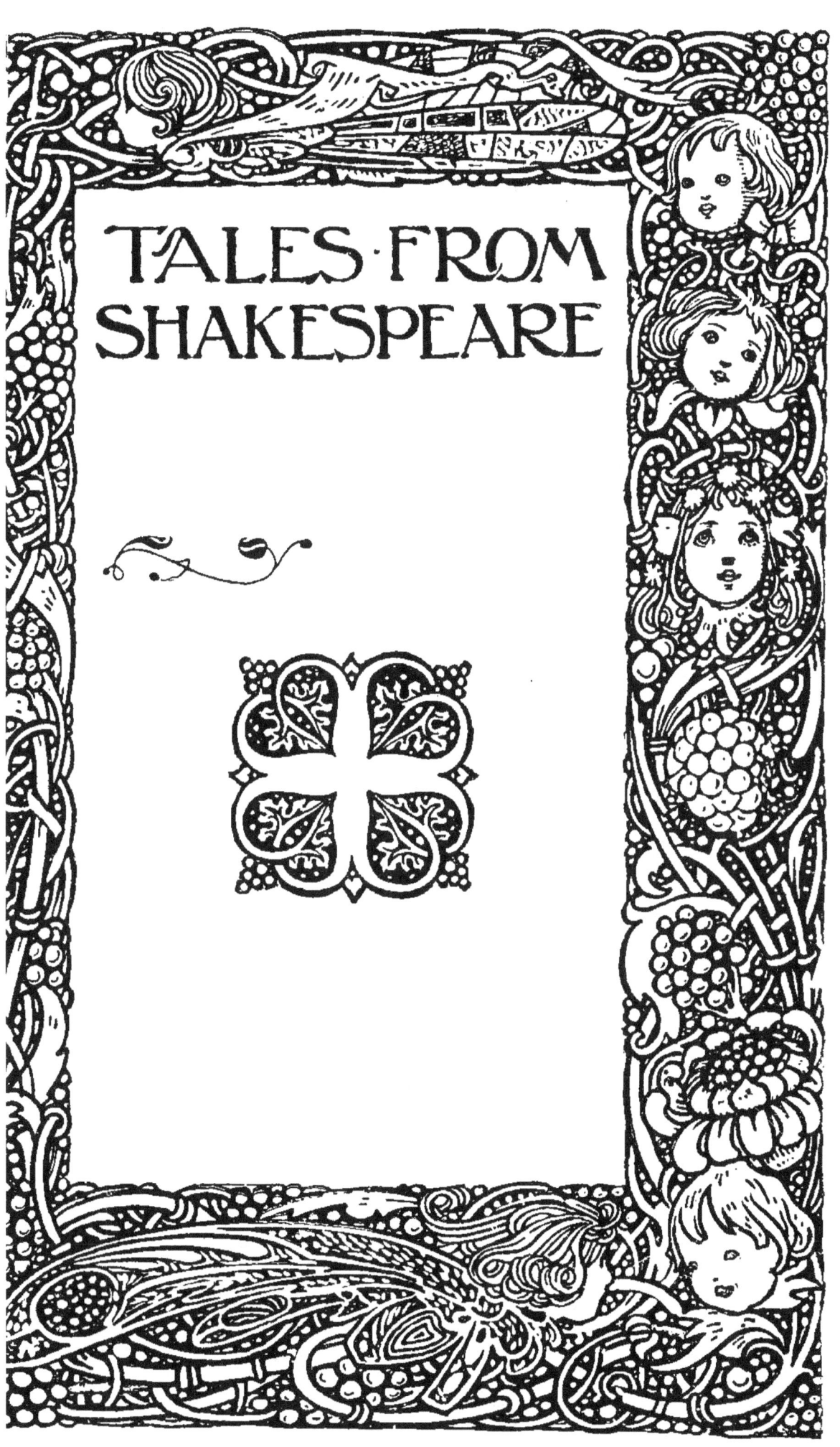

TALES·FROM SHAKESPEARE

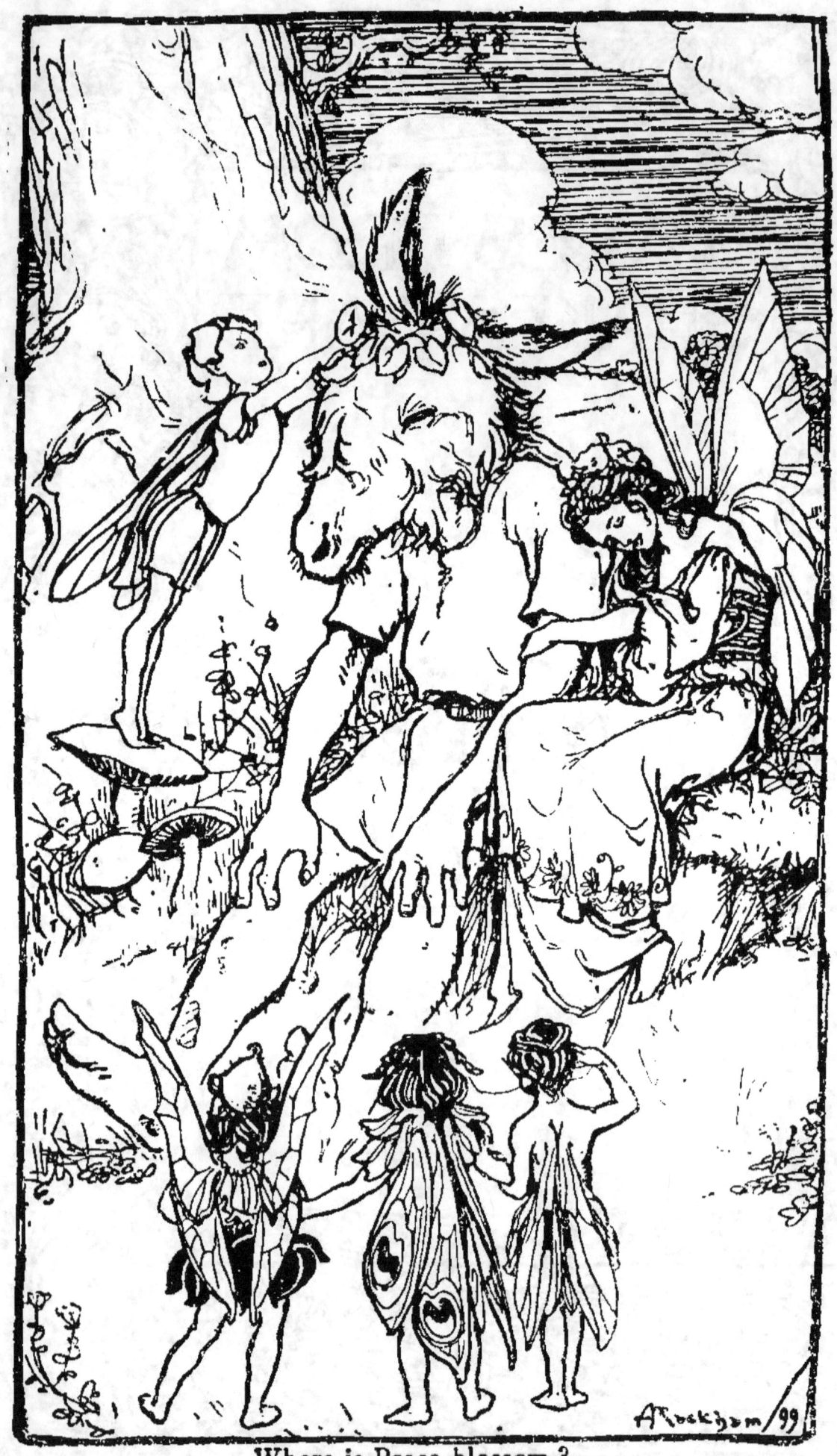

Where is Pease-blossom?

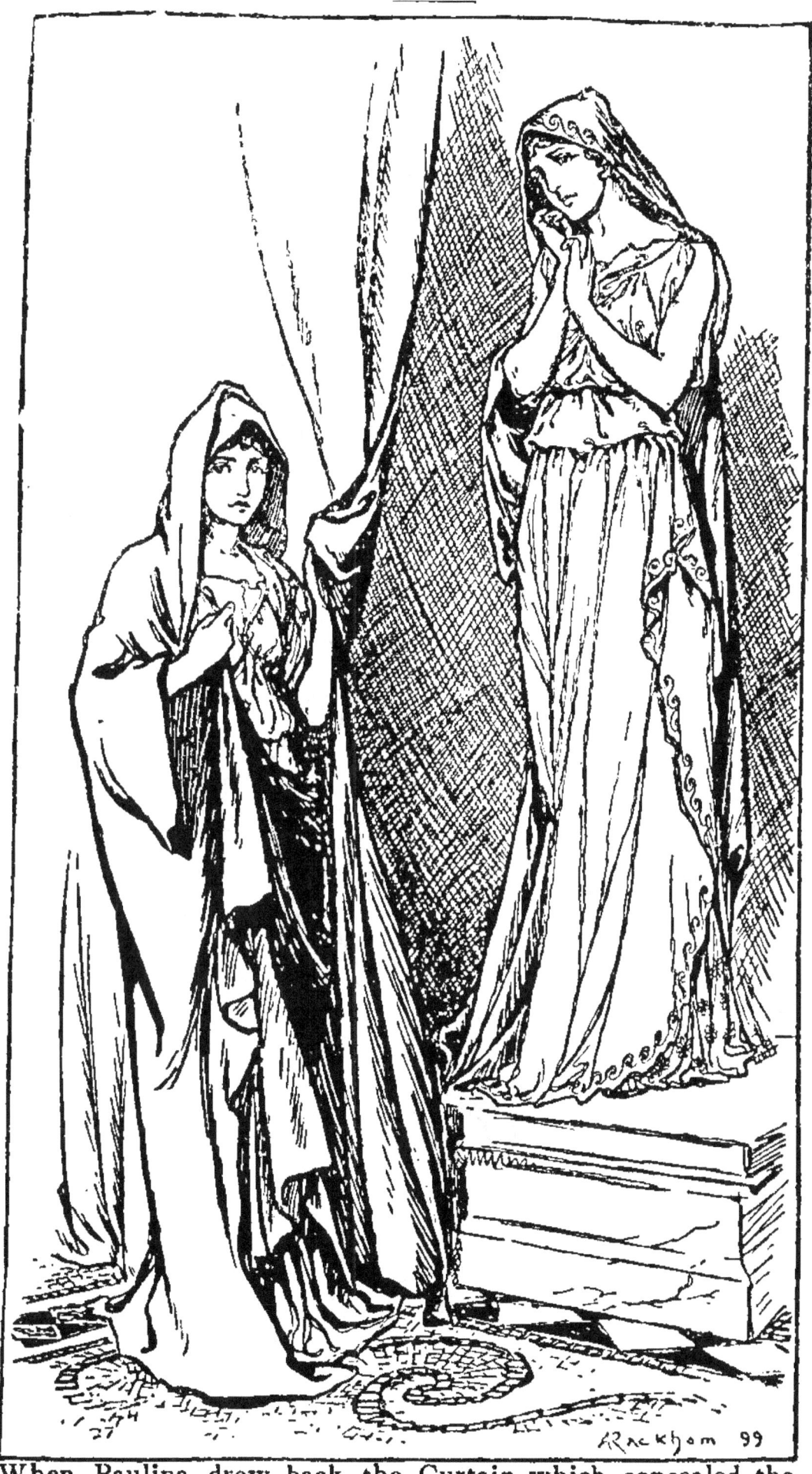
When Paulina drew back the Curtain which concealed the famous Statue.

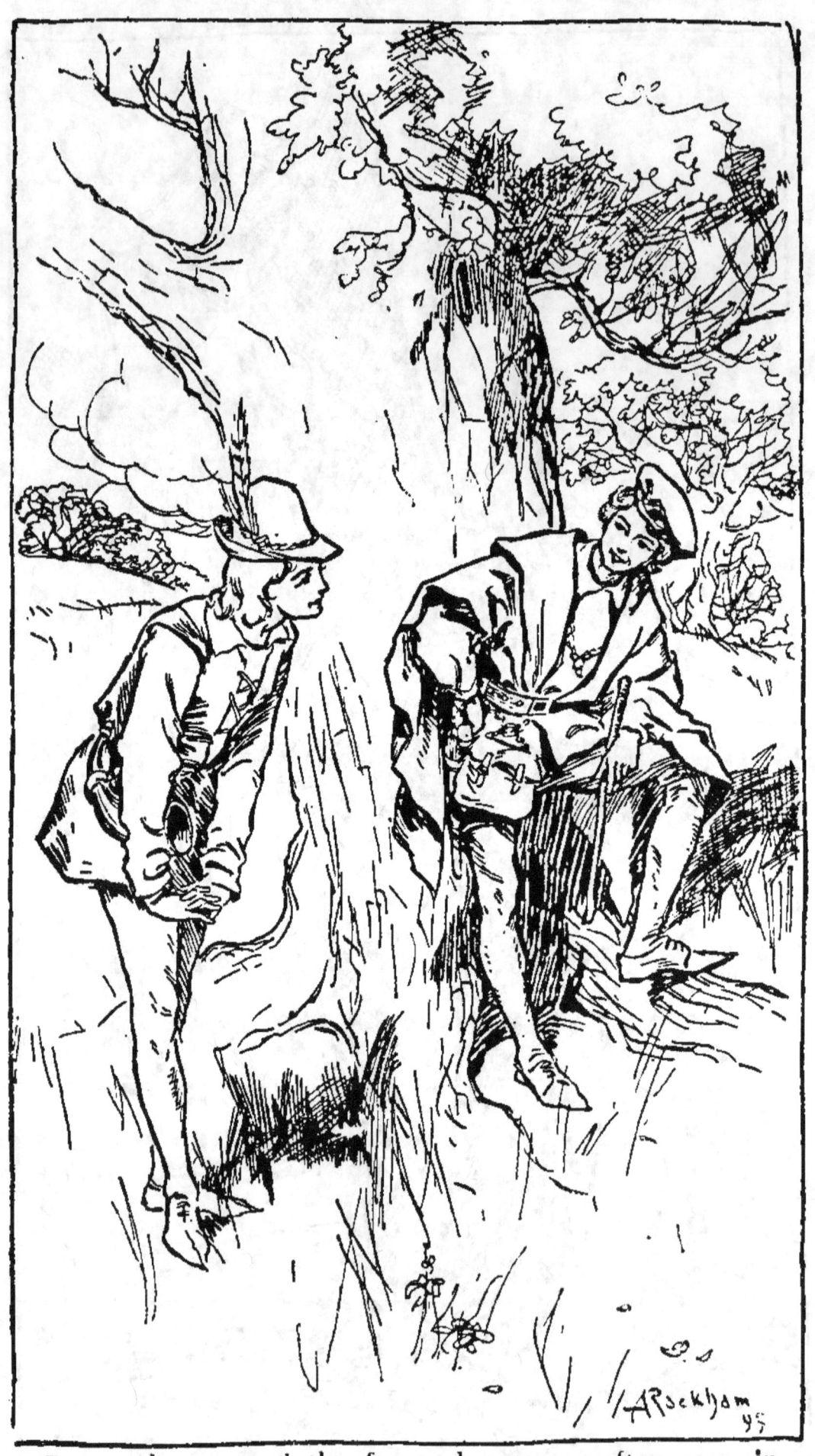

Ganymede assumed the forward manners often seen in youths when they are between boys and men.

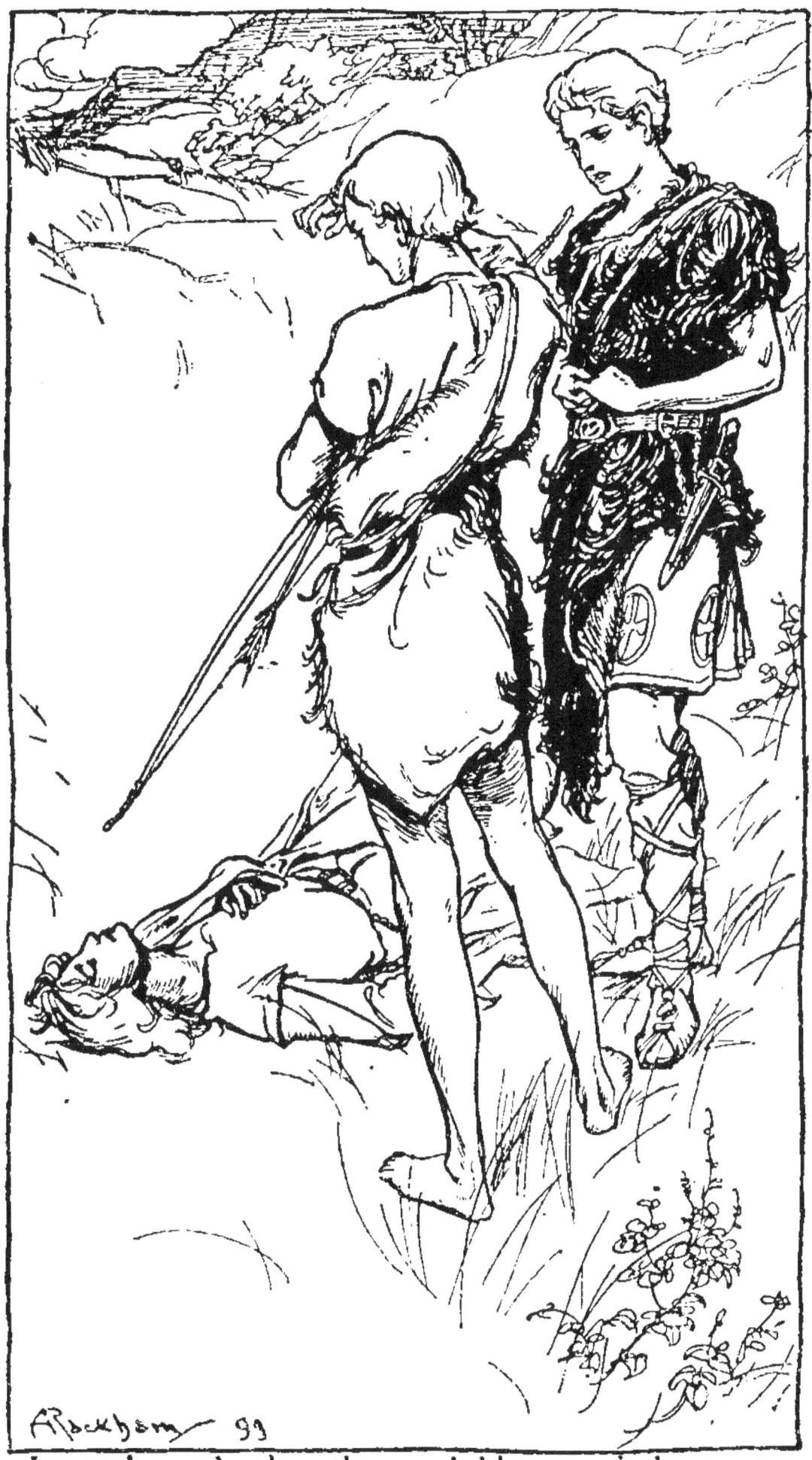

Imogen's two brothers then carried her to a shady covert.

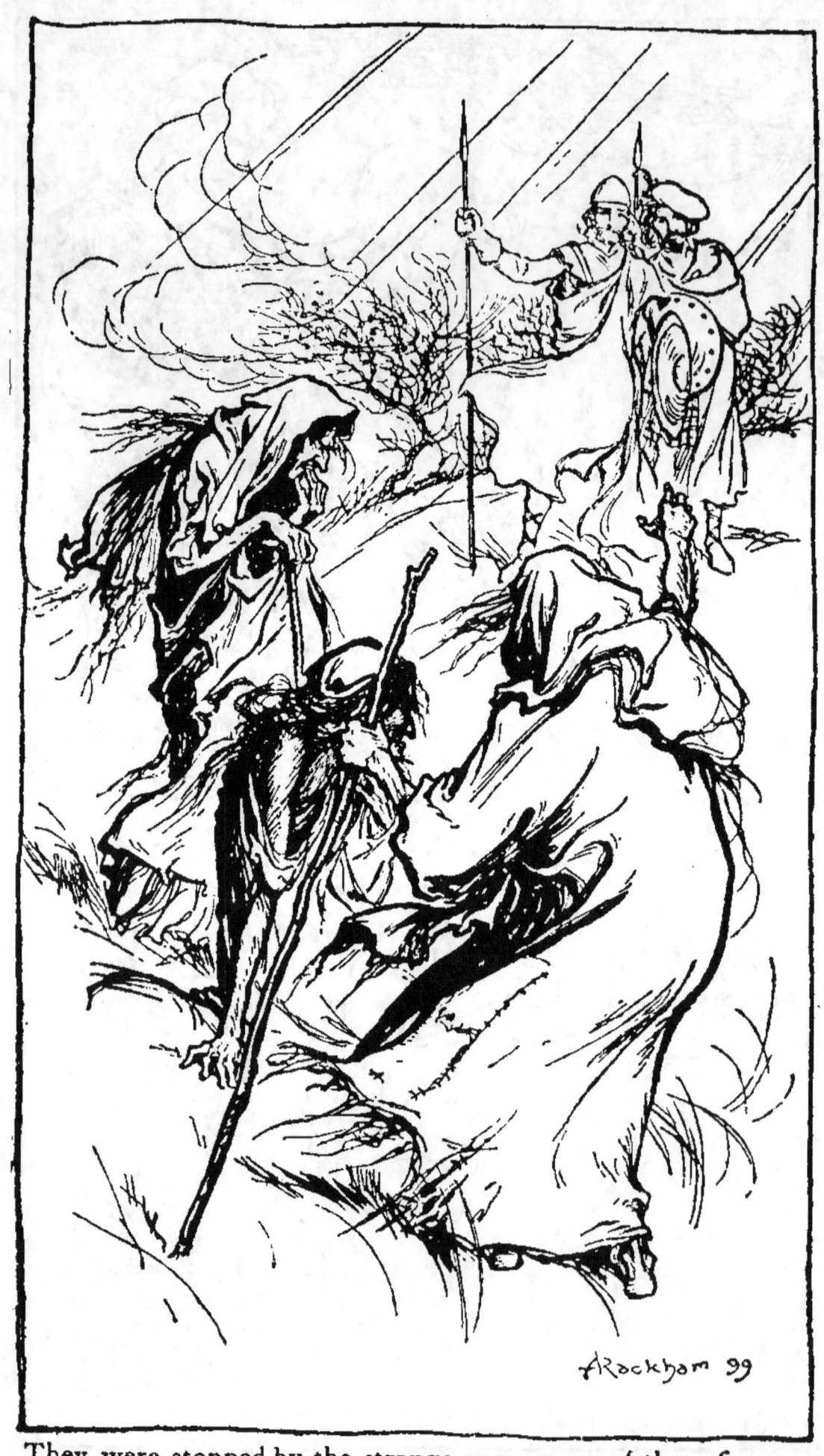

They were stopped by the strange appearance of three figures.

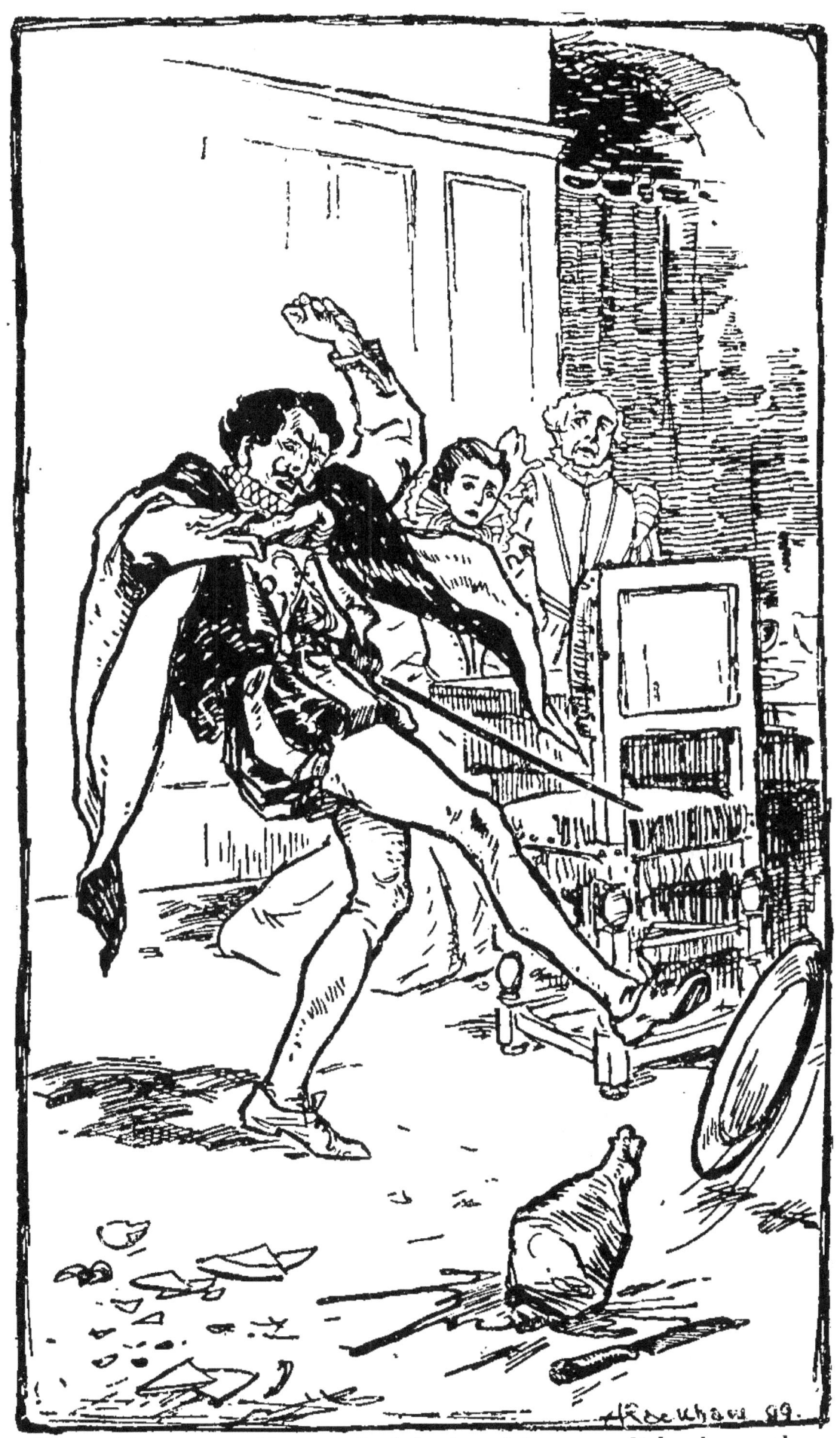

Petruchio, pretending to find fault with every dish, threw the meat about the floor

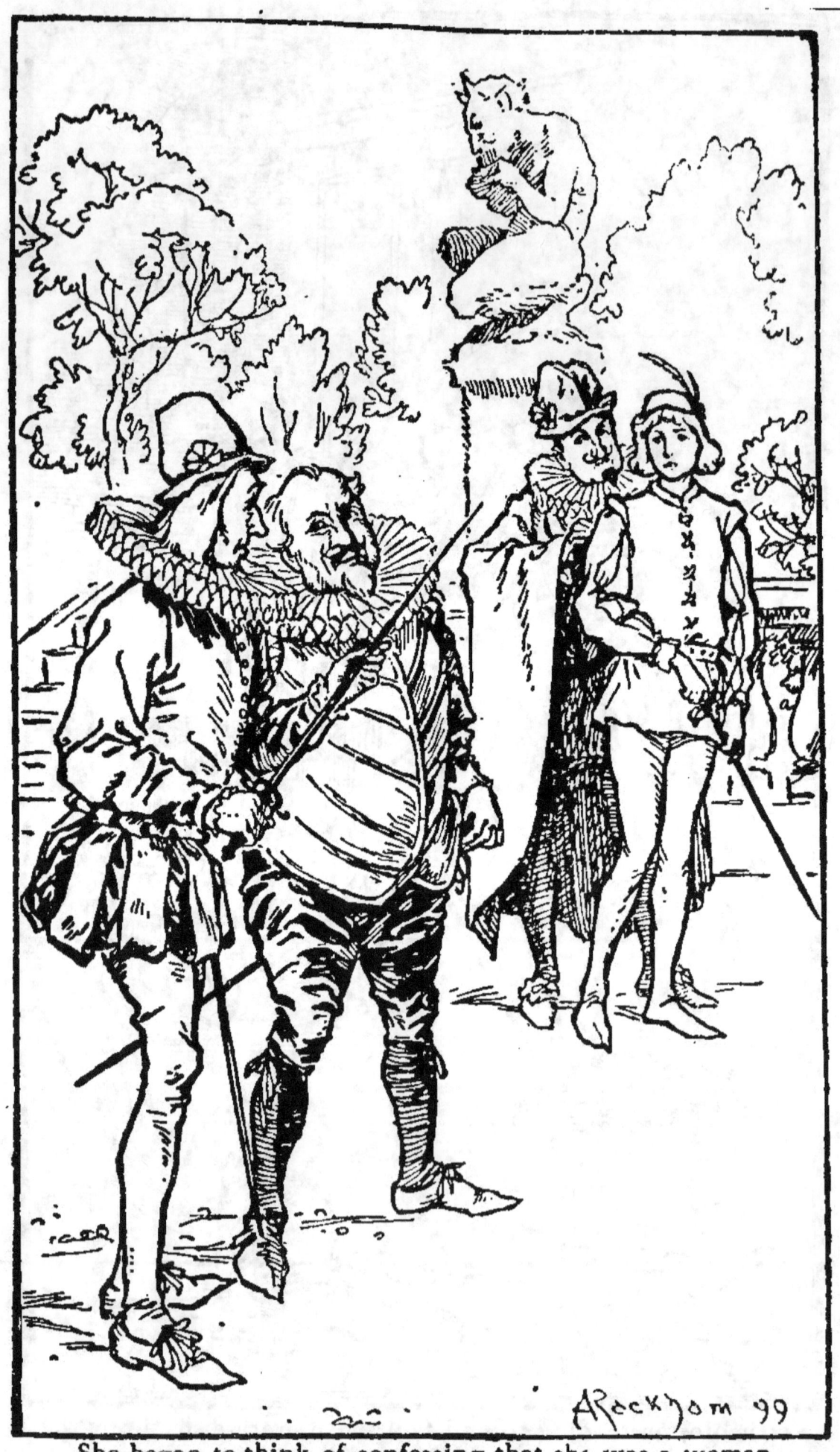

She began to think of confessing that she was a woman.

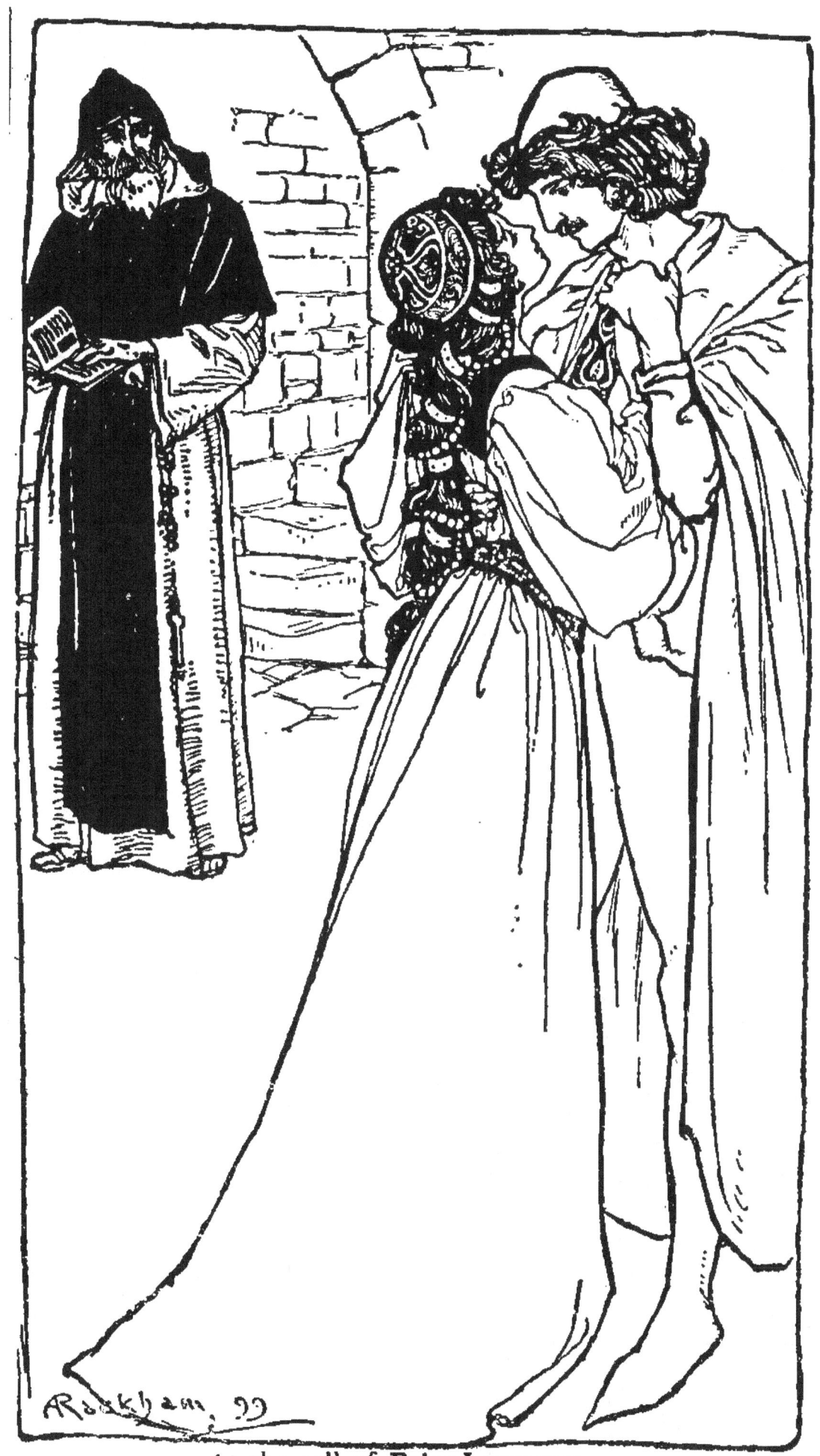

At the cell of Friar Lawrence.

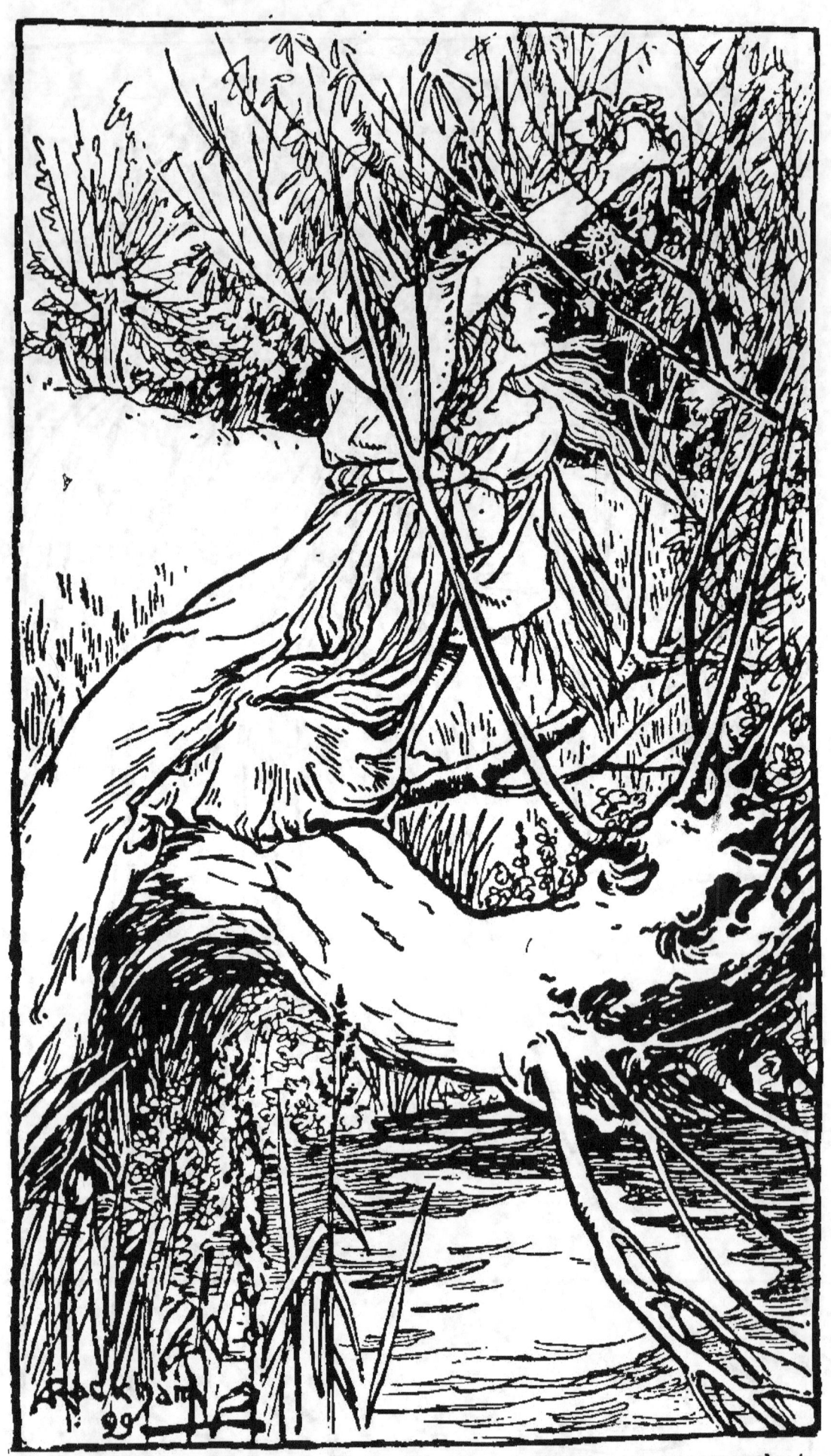

To this brook Ophelia came one day when she was unwatched.

www.ingramcontent.com/pod-product-compliance
Lightning Source LLC
Chambersburg PA
CBHW082125220526
45472CD00009D/2303